D1583227

HAROLD'S
HUNGRY EYES

For Alannah

Phaidon Press Limited
Regent's Wharf
All Saints Street
London N1 9PA

Phaidon Press Inc.
65 Bleecker Street
New York, NY 10012

phaidon.com

First published 2016
© 2016 Phaidon Press Limited
Text and illustration copyright © Kevin Waldron

Artwork created with pen, acrylic,
collage and digitally rendered.
Typeset in Purple Regular.

ISBN 978 0714 87124 0
008-0316

Designed by Meagan Bennett

Printed in China

HAROLD'S HUNGRY EYES

by Kevin Waldron

Harold was hungry.
Harold was insatiably hungry.

All
of
the
time.

After a filling meal, Harold
would lick his bowl clean . . .

go out for a walk . . .

... then get home to his comfy chair
and dream of delicious things!

his left side,

He would lie on his right side,

belly-up,

or paws down,
but *always* in
the same chair.

Harold loved his chair . . .
almost as much as he loved food.

One morning, Harold was on his way
to eat breakfast when he stopped short —
his chair had disappeared!

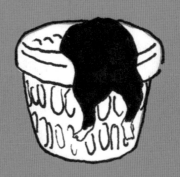

Poor Harold searched his home from top to bottom, but his chair was nowhere to be found.

Just as he lost all hope, there was a loud noise outside.
Harold peered out of the window.

There it was!
His chair!

Without a second thought, Harold squeezed out of the window and leapt down to the ground.

But he was too late — the chair was in the
truck, and the truck was speeding away!

Harold's little legs were no match for
those big wheels, and he soon lost sight
and scent of the truck.

Now his chair was gone . . .

. . . and Harold was LOST!
Where was he? Which way
was home?

Harold didn't know.
He had never been outside
by himself before.

Just then, Harold's tummy began to r-u-u-u-mble.

Harold hadn't had his breakfast!

Now all he could think about was FOOD and finding his way back home.

As he wandered the streets, Harold saw lots
of delicious things. He stopped to lick his lips,
but his empty belly urged him on.

Suddenly, Harold came across something
that he recognized from his walks.

All at once, Harold knew where he was!

Harold broke into a run.

He was so close to home, he could taste it!

Home
at
last!

Harold thoroughly enjoyed
his breakfast . . . until he
remembered that his chair
was gone.

So he could hardly believe his eyes when he saw —

— something even better.

Was Harold dreaming? He had
a brand-new place to lie down,
and it was PERFECT!

But it would have to wait.
"Haaaar-rold! Walkies!"

Leabharlanna Poiblí Chathair Baile Átha Cliath

Dublin City Public Libraries

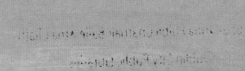